The Book

Johan Boshoff

Touch of Life International Foundation

The Book

ISBN-10: 1-62664-178-1
ISBN-13: 978-1-62664-178-5

Copyright © 2018 by **Touch of Life International Foundation.** NPO 2016/031478/08
All rights reserved
10. 5th Cresent
Campell Town
Mount Edgecome
Durban
South Africa

E-mail Address: johan@touchoflife.org.za
Web Address: www.touchoflife.org.za

1st Printing February 2018

Published by **Apostolic Movement International, LLC**
Web Address: www.ami-bookshop.com

All rights reserved under International Copyright Law. Contents may not be reproduced in whole or in part in any form without the express written consent of the publisher.

Unless specified, all Scripture references taken from THE HOLY BIBLE, NEW INTERNATIONAL VERSION®, NIV® Copyright © 1973, 1978, 1984, 2011 by Biblica, Inc.®
Used by permission. All rights reserved worldwide.

I have known Johan for probably 20 years now. During that time, he has stayed faithful to God, despite some serious personal challenges. This book comes out of the depths of his being, not the tips of his fingers, and has an urgency about it that wants to pour into and help others. Most people will find some part resonating within their hearts.

Pastor Andre Olivier
Rivers Church, South Africa

Foreword

No one can walk the road that the Lord has put you on, because your journey is unique. As you page through each principle in this book, realize that a new road spans before you. Ask yourself, "How will I walk it?" With years of experience in the missionary field and hands-on work with leaders all over the world, Johan condenses and explains the footsteps every single one of us makes as we head out into the world.

Whether you have served the Lord for years or are just starting out, one thing is made clear - this is your journey. You must decide how you will walk it, and the clear instructions here will give you a guideline to ensure that you continue to move forward as the Lord Jesus leads you a step at a time.

Colette Toach
Apostle and Co-Founder
Apostolic Movement International

Why *The Book*

In the English language, the word "the" carries with it the weight of something being extremely important. The word "book" is derived from the Indo-European Germanic root, which means beech tree.

Placing these two words side by side signals out the importance and longevity your life can and should experience. This should inspire you to stir up within yourself a passion and determination to dig yourself out of the deepest hole that life throws at you and help you to continue soaring into the heights of a freed life, just like the eagles above us.

The Book is the beginning of restoration for your life while you discover the purpose that Father God has for you.

After all, if your vehicle is broken, you take it to the manufacturer who knows how the vehicle should work. God created you in your mother's womb and gave you life. It's time to seek your Creator's help. Only He can truly diagnose and give you the transformational solutions.

Your life is also *The Book*, which will remain in the minds and hearts of those left behind once your last page is written. What story will your pages contain? I hope to be the one God uses to challenge and encourage you to begin to fill your pages with experiences of greater contentment, increased influence, and abundant inner peace.

Contents

Foreword 4

Why *The Book* 6

Chapter 01 – The Book 12

Chapter 02 – My Journey..................... 22

Chapter 03 – Lesson Learnt 30

   Submission to Spiritual Authority 32

   Forgiveness 37

   Live for Today..................................... 39

   Smile 41

   Passion and Purpose.......................... 45

   Humility.. 48

   Pray and Read Your Bible.................. 52

Chapter 04 – What are you Going to Do?
.... 62

About the Author 65

Acknowledgements 67

Chapter 01

The Book

Chapter 01 - The Book

Late one summer's day, the sight that I saw unfold before my eyes sent a message from my mind to my foot to ease up on the gas pedal, slow down, and stop on the side of the road. I had never before seen this sight and have never had the privilege to see it again.

I was in a landlocked country, known one time in history to have been the breadbasket of Africa. I had taken some time out of my schedule to take a short journey out of town, just to have some alone time.

I love the open African landscapes, the fresh, dry smell of dust and thorn trees, covered from branch to branch with the most enchanting spider webs. From a distance, the webs were spun with brilliant, structural skill, but upon closer inspection, it was a death trap for those who would wander and linger too close to the unseen danger.

In this natural environment where I escaped for time to reflect and communicate with my Maker, the sight that unfolded before me was so naturally glorious and full of splendor. Only the Creator of Heaven and Earth could have arranged this moment in time, just for me, so I felt.

I have come to fully understand that when a human heart is committed to communicate with Father God, He too is ready and willing to have a conversation with you. "If you seek me with your whole heart," God said, "you will find me."

Remember, my purpose for this short adventure was to reflect and communicate with my Maker.

As I opened my car door and placed my right foot ever so gently onto the dust, followed by my left foot, I felt as if I was standing on holy ground.

Dust particles lifted as weight shifted between my feet, inviting the slight breeze to cover my shoes with fine dust. But, my gaze was skyward, captivated with what unfolded before me.

To my right was this magnificent sun just off ground level, almost close enough to reach out and touch it in its completeness. It was massive in size and a blazing mixture of reds and yellows. Behind it was a clear blue sky, not a cloud in sight.

Immediately to my left was another captivating sight - the moon in its full glory, directly in line with the sun, just as close.

There were these two light makers that were directly opposite each other, the moon drawing her energy from the sun. The moon shone a translucent white, with a clear blue sky behind her, making her appearance of even greater significance.

There I was, captivated, in awe and standing alone in the presence of this natural display of life and sustenance. Yet, my heart was pounding, having a very clear understanding in my spirit that this was a setup by the Creator of Heaven and Earth. I was caught in this moment of time, just like Peter and John on the Mount of transfiguration. God was responding to my deepest desire and my longing to communicate with Him.

I stood still with only my neck moving my head from right to left, my eyes absorbing every second of this unfolding extravagance of a God-making.

It was as if the sun and moon had been ordered to stand on show in this position and not ascend or descend as was required by natural laws. God wanted my attention, and God got my full attention. Time stood still just for this man because he wanted to speak to God.

As I viewed the sun and moon, my attention was drawn to the long straight road between these two light suppliers for Earth. Then I heard the voice of the Lord etch these words in my spirit, which have then guided me for the rest of my life.

"As you see the road disappear in the distance, the final destination beyond eyesight, so your life has a final destination. You cannot see the end, but you must know that my Spirit is brightening your journey. Just as time has stood still for you to experience the splendor of the sun and moon, so you are to reflect my splendor as you travel through your life. Things will happen, but you will end up at the destination that I have pre-planned for you from before the creation of this world."

As I watched, listening to the changing sounds from the late afternoon into this new early evening, the sun began to fall away gently behind the horizon as the moon rose and the blue sky began to take on its darker night covering.

There I stood in solitude, with the moon giving a bright, yet gentle, warm light to expose and display the thorn trees in the background and used my body to cast the beginning of a lonely shadow. I had achieved and experienced far more than I had hoped for when I had left town.

I got back into the car, sat for a moment as my heart, mind, and spirit recalled everything that had taken place. God had chosen to not just speak to me, but He had instructed His creation to formulate a natural picture that would remain with me for the rest of this life on earth.

The combination of the voice of the living God and His creation had solidified a moment of communication that has kept me going straight towards my destination. This once-in-a-lifetime changing moment happened almost thirty years ago, and it's just as fresh today as when it happened.

In writing this book, I want you to be inspired, encouraged, and motivated to never give up on yourself or the living Christ.

Your life is extremely important to you and everyone else that will cross your journey. I made it short by intention, so that you can read it while traveling on a plane, having your lunch, or in your darkest moments of life. You need to lift yourself up and achieve your full potential in this life.

During your life, you too have had God speak to you through a life circumstance, picture, or through a conversation with someone. But then, you did not recognize or acknowledge Him. I invite you, as you engage with the following pages, to revisit that special moment and recommit to live your life with a new determination and zeal.

Chapter 02

My Journey

Chapter 02 - My Journey

I am a son of the African soil, born in the middle of Africa, in a country now called Zambia. My parents lived a simple but happy life, which helped me to know contentment but yet reach for the purposes of Christ.

As life continued, my father was transferred to the country now known as Zimbabwe. There I spent a number of years completing my schooling and was constricted to spend four years of my life protecting the ideals of a minority group who were eventually instructed to surrender to a majority.

It was here that my love for Christ began to grow. It was normal during those early years to be church attendees, commit to public events to gather people from across the church spectrum, and celebrate Christ and evangelize the local communities.

Just after my marriage, I was transferred to South Africa to work in a company that required the skills and expertise that I had been trained for. This move in the Father's purpose stirred a deep thirst and desire to further educate myself. I became a student of both commerce and Biblical studies.

Once I had received my qualifications, I progressed up the corporate ladder while my involvement in church life became even stronger. I had to eventually make a decision, after much prayer, to obey the Lord and take up His calling for my life. My journey between the sun and moon was beginning to take further shape.

I had been on a number of missionary trips and on one in particular to Zimbabwe, I felt a strong desire to start a Bible training center. After all the required documentation had been approved, my family and I relocated back to Zimbabwe.

Here we spent a number of years, heading up the Bible school, establishing extension schools, and pastoring a church, which I had attended as a young boy.

The Lord knew my journey and was training me in the ministry. Training at most times is tough. We faced many difficulties and disappointments with severe family trauma, but with our Father's help, we came through everything. Our permitted time had come to an end, and we had to move back to South Africa.

This opened another door for me to pastor a church, and later, I was relocated still again to another church in a different province. Each time this happened, the experience I had had in those early days was brought back to my mind, and my heart would become expectant again.

The words rang in my spirit, "...you cannot see your final destination, but know I am with you".

It was during a time of much growth in the local church and increased influence in the local and regional community that I would have to face one of the darkest experiences of my life.

We faced a family trauma that almost broke the family apart. My wife of almost thirty years just left and walked out of our life, never to return. But the light of

Christ, the support of colleges, spiritual leaders, and prophetic words from around the world, carried us through to a place of stability and renewed productivity for the Kingdom.

Because of constitutional requirements of the denomination I belonged to, I had to step away from the local church as Senior Pastor and take up a possible situation elsewhere on staff.

Remember, God had spoken to me years before that I wouldn't see the destination but that He is watching me. Well, during this time of transition, the Lord opened an opportunity for me to submit to another ministry with my denomination's blessing - to support and develop evangelism and discipleship in Africa.

What a life-changing experience I was given for The Kingdom! God does know your life's journey.

In my tenth year of serving another man's vision, the Spirit of God began speaking to me about leaving the success that I was enjoying and to step out of Africa onto another continent.

Once again faced with another God opportunity, we prayed, fasted, sought counsel, and obeyed. After being released by the ministry with the founder's blessing, we relocated to another region of the country and began giving our lives in obedience for ministering in Asia.

I said we. During my years with the evangelism ministry, I had met a godly woman who was also working in a different department of the ministry. We submitted our relationship to those we were under and got married. Now we are traveling in Asia, mentoring, encouraging, and ministering the Good News to people also loved by God.

Chapter 03

Lesson Learnt

Chapter 03 - Lesson Learnt

The road that you have been called to walk on could be similar to mine, or indeed, very different. However, I have discovered throughout my journey that the decisions we make on our journey can open God opportunities or cause us to wander off track and into some sticky situations that can cause deep pain and regret.

Again, let me make mention of the fact that Father God does and wants to speak to every human heart. We are, however, responsible to give Him the time to speak while we just listen.

In today's climate of instant gratification, there are life lessons that still remain and need to take priority and be worked through in your life should you desire to reach the end of your journey with a complete knowing of fulfillment and a sense of pleasure that you have given to Father God.

Here are seven lessons that I have learnt that I know will help you achieve your God-given destiny. Take one a week and work it through into your personal DNA and then start over again.

In each time of processing, each principle will reveal a deeper and satisfying influence in your life, calling the world around you to open up doors of opportunities for blessing and favor.

Submission to Spiritual Authority

The Bible is very clear on this point. Submission gives you protection and authority to live out your godly purpose.

To illustrate this lesson, let me tell you of two intensely grave situations I had to walk through. The first being, I was still just beginning on this road of ministry, serving as an elder in a local church.

We had a guest speaker one Sunday who was very charismatic in his delivery and so was well received by the congregation. However, the Monday following, I was asked to attend a meeting with this guest speaker and the pastor.

I arrived with excitement as to why I would be called. Little did I know that my life was going to change in an instant. At the end of a very short meeting, I was instructed to resign as an elder and have no part in the church going forward as the guest speaker had influenced the pastor that I had another agenda. What a shock to my system.

The following Sunday, I was called up in front of the church with the false accusation used to discredit me. Half the members got up and left. I, in turn, standing before the people and pastor I had served faithfully, made a decision that the Holy Spirit directed me into (because, left to my flesh, the outcome would have certainly been different).

Knowing my innocence in this matter, the Spirit said to remain steadfast, don't leave, and continue to support the church for as long as it takes.

During the following six months, I was encouraged to leave the church (from members who had left that Sunday). Some even became angry at my disapproval of their actions. But, because I was under the instruction of the Holy Spirit, and under submission to Him, I continued faithfully in the weekly prayer meeting as well as every Sunday service.

Needless to say that my presence at the meetings was, let's just say, very uncomfortable, but I was under submission to the Holy Spirit's instruction.

With everything that took place, if I wrote it all down you would be reading this for the next month, so let me get to the end. After one Sunday morning, as I walked out of the service into the car park, there was a shattering in the spiritual realm.

I suddenly felt the massive burden that I had been carrying just fall off me. I felt so extremely light - light enough to lift off the ground.

At that precise moment, when the pastor was greeting the other members at the church door, he experienced the same spiritual exchange that took place. Our eyes caught sight of each other, knowing that something had just happened.

The next day, I was called and asked for forgiveness, privately and publicly. Some years later, the Lord used that pastor to ordain me into full-time ministry.

The second occasion where I had to submit to authority was when I was told to step down and away from being the Senior Pastor because of the trauma that my children and I had experienced. Here again, many congregation members spoke to me about remaining, with the intention of removing themselves from the denomination so that I could continue being their pastor.

But since my journey years before had taken me through a very dark place where I was taught to remain under submission, I responded without any question. I submitted to the denomination's leadership, and the rest of my journey gives testimony to being under authority.

Hence, I understand and fully appreciate the grace of God upon my life. The long road on which I have traveled gives me opportunities to look back, reflect and gage my progress, which has become my anchor, my hope, and security in Christ.

> ***Hebrews 13.17.*** *Obey your leaders and submit to them, for they are keeping watch over your souls, as those who will have to give an account. (ESV)*

Forgiveness

Not just forgiving individuals who have caused the deepest pain in your life, but forgiving unconditionally. Not forgiveness with a condition tied to it. Also, forgive yourself. You are human and not perfect. You also need to release yourself from the pain and disappointments that life throws at you. Most of the disappointments are created to get you distracted from reaching your God-given journey's end.

Having a mental understanding of forgiveness and having a heart that lives forgiveness are poles apart. It's similar to individuals who have head knowledge about Christ, but their heart and character have never been renewed.

During my experience of being falsely accused, I had to discover the inner reality of forgiveness, without any restrictions placed on those I had chosen to forgive.

Although my human nature and cultural upbringing would have justified any other acceptable response and actions of retribution as normal by human standards, that did not align itself to my Heavenly Father's agenda.

I learnt that His agenda of forgiveness without restriction is the only path towards the healing of my soul. The phrase, used by many struggling through life, "I forgive you, but..." will never be sufficient to attract healing to your own heart.

Forgiveness is extremely important for your own well-being and health to successfully complete your book.

> ***Matthew 6.12 and 14.*** *And forgive us our debts, as we also have forgiven our debtors.*
>
> *For if you forgive other people when they sin against you, your heavenly Father will also forgive you.*

Live for Today

Every day you open your eyes could be your last in your journey. Make wise decisions to enjoy it. Enjoy it by being open to serve others, and be thankful and content with what you have.

Too many people arrive at their journey's end, discovering that they have not truly lived a full life, but only existed to survive a daily routine of do's and don'ts.

Being fearful of leaving the known security to explore their inner desires of adventure on foreign shores. Taking that must needed family time. Creating those lasting memories caught on all the electronic devices available today.

Although useful, no electronic device can give you the emotions, the feelings, the smells of green grass staining your knees as you roll around with your family. Only your emotions have the capacity to store up such valuable well-spent hours.

Speak to the person who waited upon your table, ask them what their name means, and take an interest in their life.

The investment of interest into their world will give you a return, a harvest of joy and contentment that you also lived for someone else.

Tomorrow never really becomes a reality. If you arrive there, it's already today! So today, use your life on the section of journey you are on to enjoy every moment. Why waste your precious commodities of time and heart emotion to get and remain bitter and unforgiving?

Enjoy today as you share your life with others.

> ***1 Thessalonians 5.13.*** *Live in peace with each other.*

Smile

Yes, this simple but extremely important action will open opportunities into the worlds of those you meet along your journey. Your smile could be the message that someone contemplating taking their life is looking for, not to end their life.

It has been said that to understand the cover of a book, you need to discover its content, page after page. So it is with all those faces we encounter through our journey. Each face carefully sculptured so that it hides with the intention of deflecting attention away from depths of pain, discontentment, and insecurities that have been accepted as normal.

Your willingness to be vulnerable, open-faced, willing to invest one of your most valuable asset, time, just to smile at someone. Your smile from a pure, honest heart has the power to transform a person's life journey.

Come with me, as I take you into the world of an individual who stands for hours every day behind a counter, serving people. Every hour of every day, she looks into faces, who themselves are caught up in negativity, sadness, urgency, perhaps even rudeness.

Imagine what she must be feeling like at the end of her day. Already discouraged, tired, and perhaps broken down by those she served, she must now take up her own private journey with her own struggles.

It is no wonder that many a customer would pass a comment, something like, "That assistant is so unfriendly". But little do they understand that those she has had to serve before they came along have adversely influenced that counter assistant's attitude. All day long, there has been a transfer of feelings and emotions from customers to this counter assistant.

Now, there you arrive, standing on the opposite side of the counter, with a pure heart and an ear open to the voice of the Spirit. You smile and tell her she has a nice smile. Even though her face is as stern as brass, she looks up at you, and her face softens. Her eyes light up. You, in turn, hear the Spirit say, "Tell her that the problem you left at home will be sorted because God loves her." You instantly obey.

Suddenly, everything that that assistant carried from home, all the negativity transferred to her, disappears in one second as mist burned away from the sun's heat. Tears begin to roll down her cheeks, drawing lines through her make up. Her face displays a tenderness, and her voice trembles with sincere appreciation, "Thank you Sir. You just changed my life".

It cost you nothing to smile, but your smile and obedience radically transformed a person's journey. Your name will never be known, but your smile will be remembered way after you are no more.

> ***Proverbs 15.13.*** *A happy heart makes the face cheerful.*

Passion and Purpose

Every day, serve God and those around you with passion and purpose.

Many books have been written about passion and purpose. Individuals have become financially secure from using these two driving forces to motivate conference attendees.

Passion, a compelling emotion combined with purpose, a strong determination to achieve something significant in your journey, should be your objective.

As my journey between the sun and the moon unfolded, it took me to serve another man's vision for evangelizing Africa. What an awesome vision. My part was to develop the teams and extend his vision into as many countries as the resources became available. My responsibility was simple - fully understand the heart of the visionary and execute what the Lord had birthed in his heart.

As I co-owned the vision, my emotions were stirred by the vastness of Africa and the potential of the souls that could be reached with the gospel. My determination, along with the team I had, to serve and develop created a deep desire to achieve the visionary's mandate from God.

It became my total focus. It not only used my energies but also was a well of fresh water, restoring the energy required to achieve the set objectives.

Your journey needs to evoke deep, compelling emotions that fuel within a determination to achieve the very best you can do in serving others. Even if you are in the position where you don't report to anyone, you must always be ready to have passion and purpose accompany you.

Perhaps if more husbands and wives, fathers and mothers engage compelling emotions and determination in their marriage and family life, life might become just that more satisfying and enjoyable.

> ***Proverbs 16.3.*** *Commit your actions to the Lord, and your plans will succeed. (NLT)*

Humility

This is maybe one of those qualities that are not spoken of with much appreciation today, but without it, your journey will be a lot harder to accomplish. Many associate humility with weakness, shyness, or insecurity. This, dear reader, is so far from the reality.

Authentic humility is grounded in knowing who you are, without having to constantly perform or prove yourself to those you engage with. I like to use the phrase, "You must be comfortable in your skin." Being comfortable in your skin gives you an inner strength and confidence to conduct your life with contentment.

As I stood in the dust, awestruck with the sun and moon's display of glory and splendor, it was as though I was standing on holy ground, the reality of an Almighty God. The Creator of Heaven and Earth and these two powerful magnificent producers of life-sustainers through their combined functions to give off light, for the wellbeing of the inhabitants of Earth and nature's cycles of cold, warmth, sowing and harvesting.

There I stood, a very small extension of the dust from which I had been created, being spoken to by the Creator. Humbling indeed. This life-changing experience has helped me to understand that my life is but a breath away from disappearing from the face of the Earth into eternity with Christ.

To be falsely accused in a public meeting, to step away from a thriving ministry is an extremely humiliating experience for anyone to go through. But to decide to stay true to what God had birthed in your heart and mind will help you continue your journey towards the destination that God has ordained just for you.

Knowing who you are in Christ will reinforce within you a capacity to surrender your pride and personal rights at these difficult times. Authentic humility empowers you to recognize and deal with the twin emotions of pride and self-importance.

When these emotions are not recognized and dealt a deathblow, they will spoil your journey with self-destruction, causing deep recurring pain to yourself and others.

God etched on my heart that I was to display His splendor during my journey and that I would someday reach my destination. Knowing who I am in Christ has developed in me this capacity to surrender my egotistic emotions, to have a healthier and productive journey.

Through your journey, opportunities will be placed before you to display from your heart a humble attitude, or a stubbornness to be right. Recognizing these negative and self-destructive attitudes is like the red warning lights that flash on your vehicle's dashboard, "Danger, something is wrong!"

It's time to make an urgent pit stop on your journey and inquire of the Lord. What does He have in mind for you, and what must you do to resolve your negative and self-destructive attitudes?

> ***Philippians 2.3.*** *Rather, in humility value others above yourselves*

Pray and Read Your Bible

Although I have placed this on the bottom of the lesson list, this activity is by far the most important. Without hearing the voice of the Spirit and reading scripture, you will be eroding yourself of blessings and favor that the Lord has already prepared for you.

If I were to ask you what you had for dinner last year August, I think that it would be difficult to recall exactly what you had. However, so it is with most of your meals. You could remember the favorite meals but not the others.

The point here is, you are alive now and reading this book because, along your journey of life, you had to take in substance of some sort. Some of it was extremely beneficial while others were detrimental to your health, because your desire overruled your good sense.

This same principle applies to the spiritual part of our journey. Unless you have a photographic mind, you might not remember what you read a few weeks ago, but just the fact that you took time to invest into your spiritual well-being. When required, the Spirit of God will give you recall of a certain scripture, to reinforce your conviction and commitment when something unforeseen makes its appearance on your journey of life.

As we began this journey together, I mentioned that when your vehicle is broken, you take it to the manufacturer. So, we too need to inquire from our manufacturer to diagnose our problem and give us the correct solution. The wisest person who ever lived on earth, King Solomon, is credited with writing the book of Ecclesiastes.

In chapter 3 and verse 11, he made a statement that is like the manufacturer's emblem on the vehicle of your choice. *"He (God) has also set eternity in the human heart (human race); yet no one can fathom what God has done from beginning to end."* What a revelation! The Creator, our manufacturer, did something so unique that one else can make a forgery.

His emblem of eternity is so firmly set into every human heart. From the 18th day of conception, His emblem, eternity, is firmly set into the human heart. It is no wonder that we are instructed in the book of Proverbs chapter 4 verse 23 *"...Above all else, guard your heart, for everything you do flows from it."*.

If you choose to take your vehicle to a different manufacturer, they could repair your vehicle, but sooner or later, you will have to return to the original manufacturer to now redo what the unlicensed manufacturer did. It will now be of greater cost to repair.

Just like human nature, we make decisions that cause our journeys to take routes that our lives were never designed to take. Our health, our peace, our purity, and our total well-being suffers. Only the authorized manufacturer of the human heart can correctly diagnose and give the appropriate medication.

This is why reading the Bible every day is vital to your life journey. The life-giving words contained in the Bible of instruction, affirmation, correction, strategy, submission and healthy, wholesome living will feed your spirit.

Once your spirit is strengthened with the Bible, you will be able to face all the obstacles that make their way on your road with greater confidence.

The cousin to reading your Bible is prayer. Another word for prayer is having a conversation with Father God, similar to the way you speak to those you encounter every day. You have a native language with which you communicate your thoughts, feelings, and desires. Your Creator has a desire to speak with you about your well-being and give you special moments in time too. In your language, you just speak to Him.

I made mention that, during the darkest season of my journey, I had the support of colleges, spiritual leaders, and prophetic words. As you spend time in prayer, the Spirit of Christ can minister to you directly a word of instruction and encouragement. Or, the Lord can speak through other individuals to give you a prophetic word.

Your journey through life need not be an isolated one. You need comforters and inspirers. Just like the Apostle Paul inspired the young Timothy who was establishing a church. As recorded in 1 Timothy 1.18-19, Paul's words were reminding him to keep in line with the prophecies once made about him, so he could fight the good fight, holding on to faith and a good conscience.

A prophetic word over your life can be described as an anchor ahead of you with a rope tied securely around your waist. As you keep on praying the prophetic word, you, with God's help, will be pulling yourself through and out of your dark valleys towards the intended place of freedom and stability that God has for you.

My short journey out of town was to find solitude to speak to God. My desire was made complete. I felt totally renewed in spirit, heart, mind, and soul. Since then, I have many occasions to have meaningful discussions with the living Christ. Your personal journey too has the potential of taking on a new meaning, perhaps even a new vision for your life.

> ***Ephesians 6.18.*** *And pray in the Spirit on all occasions with all kinds of prayers and requests.*

> ***2 Timothy 2.15.*** *Do your best to present yourself to God as one approved, a worker who does not need to be ashamed and who correctly handles the word of truth.*

Chapter 04

What are you Going to Do?

Chapter 04 - What are you Going to Do?

The only person who can give authority to restructure your life, your thoughts, your character, and your success in life is you.

You have the power to begin restructuring your journey. Take those decisions that will develop within a commitment to purposefully live with conviction, guiding you to reach your ordained destination.

My hope is that I have challenged, encouraged, and motivated you to make those courageous decisions, to ensure that you too end up at the destination that God has planned for your life.

You might have been a follower of Christ and made some really bad choices in life, or you might have never actually considered up until now to make a life-changing decision.

Through this simple prayer from your heart, you can begin a new life. Your past failures (the Bible calls them sin) will be washed away because of the shed blood of Christ on the cross of Calvary. His death and resurrection after three days, which was witnessed by over five hundred individuals, gives you the confidence that Christ heard your request.

Father God, in the name of your Son Jesus Christ, I acknowledge my sin, failures, and self-centeredness. I have been hurt but have also hurt others. Please forgive my sin, and I ask Your Holy Spirit to come and live within me, teaching me your truth and way of life. Thank you, Jesus.

Dear reader, welcome into the family of the living Christ. I encourage you to find a local church near you, request a meeting with the pastor/leader, and tell him about your decision of accepting Christ Jesus as your God.

Then, make yourself available to join the church, serving the vision and become active, while enjoying renewed productivity and purposeful meaning for your life.

Romans 10.9. says that

> *If you declare with your mouth, "Jesus is Lord," and believe in your heart that God raised him from the dead, you will be saved.*
>
> *11. As Scripture says, "Anyone who believes in him will never be put to shame."*

About the Author

Johan spent the first part of his life in commerce and industry, advancing through the ranks of management. At the age of 30, after completing further studies, he was ordained in the Assemblies of God.

During his ministry years, he pastored congregations in Zimbabwe and South Africa, building close relations between the local church and community leaders. After serving 10 years as COO for an African-based evangelism ministry, he gained exposure to a number of countries in Africa.

About the Author

Following the prompting of the Holy Spirit, Johan and his wife, with another partner, established *Touch of Life International Foundation*.

Johan now travels in Asia, encouraging, mentoring, and sharing the Good News.

Johan is passionate about recognizing the potential in leaders, equipping and mentoring them, and seeing them live out their God-given talents and gifting.

Touch of Life International Foundation
South Africa
NPO Registration Number: 2016/031478/08

Read more at www.touchoflife.org.za

Acknowledgements

Pastor Anthony Minter, *Shekina Christian Church,* Benoni, South Africa

Pastor Donovan Coetzee and National Leadership, *Assemblies of God,* South Africa

Peter and Ann Pretorius, Founders of *Jesus Alive Gospel Outreach*

www.ingramcontent.com/pod-product-compliance
Lightning Source LLC
Chambersburg PA
CBHW050044080526
44586CB00014B/1454